MW00414903

PRAISE FOR THE 7 PILLARS

"The 7 Pillars" is to corporate culture, what the One Minute Manager© was to organizational management. It is a fun and enlightening read that offers sound theory but, more importantly, practical advice — examples of culture-building initiatives that readers can immediately apply within their work teams or companies. If you are looking to build a stronger and more motivating corporate culture, this book is a powerful how-to and will change the way you go about building your teams.

Gary Grimmer, Executive Chairman, GainingEdge

Dennis Campbell has come up with seven ways any company can improve. Using his unique background and illustrative examples, his ideas will resonate with any company whose leaders are ready for change that produces results. Implementing The 1ˢᵗ Pillar idea alone would be a smart move--and there are six more!

Stuart Purviance, Colonel, USAF Retired

This is a very quick read EVERY leader from Supervisor to C-Suite, experienced or new in their role, should read. "The 7 Pillars" imparts wisdom, experienced examples, and actionable takeaways in concise wording. Nicely done, Dennis.

Ed Burr, Vice President, North American On-Site LLC

*This quick, powerful read illuminates the positive approach leaders and managers should consider when building highly successful teams that perpetuate uncompromising results. With meaningful anecdotes and heartfelt strategies, Dennis Campbell's **"The 7 Pillars"** drills down on corporate buy-in that doesn't always come to managers naturally. These impactful pillars serve as a lasting reference for the seasoned mentor and successful CEO, whose goal is not only creating profit but is also rich in promoting purposeful outcomes. Culture is Key!*

M. Vander Linden, Senior Executive

*"**The 7 Pillars**" is full of fun anecdotes and team-building tips that will resonate with anybody in a leadership position, whether you are the CEO or a team leader. This is a good read even in the best of times; however, the lessons put forth in Dennis' book based on decades of real-world experience in building effective teams with a strong corporate culture have never been more important as we begin to rebuild in a post-COVID world.*

Robin Brown, Former Army Combat Helicopter Pilot & Current Executive Director, Grand Junction Economic Partnership

This book should be required reading for every mid to high-level manager in any company wanting to increase their presence. It offers a compelling argument about the importance of corporate culture as a way to increase performance. By laying out a common-sense approach and injecting personal experiences and anecdotes, Dennis makes this book both entertaining and powerful at the same time. A must-read.

Jami and Julio Gamez

THE
7 PILLARS

OF AN UNBEATABLE
COMPANY AND CULTURE

D.E. Campbell

To: Shana Abrahams —
With my compliments!
DC
7/2020

For information address Goodrich Publishing, 2425 W Bronco
Butte Trail, Unit 2020, Phoenix, AZ 85085

This book may be purchased for educational, business, or
sales promotional use. For information, please email
dcampbell@campbellra.com

Published by Goodrich Publishing
Phoenix, Arizona
GoodrichPublishing.com

ISBN-13: 978-1-7339963-3-4

TABLE OF CONTENTS

DEDICATIONS

To My Soulmate, Suzanne

Who always lifted me when I would get down or stuck in a singular gear of life, daily, and especially when I sorely needed it, you showered me with genuine and more unconditional love than I could have ever imagined existed in the world. Without your love and encouragement, this book would never be.

To My Father,

Ronald Thomas Campbell (RIP) Who gave me the gift of travel; and the experiences, teachings, and joy that comes with getting to know foreign geography, cultures, and people.

To Herb D. Kelleher (RIP) and Colleen C. Barrett,

Whose commitment to the leadership principles you championed at Southwest Airlines had the most influence on my lens and business success after Southwest and gave me purpose to help other businesses and budding leaders.

To The A-Team at Visit Albuquerque circa 1989-1996,

For the joy and experience of working with a team of wonderful human beings committed like family to a singular cause.

For My Grandchildren, Hunter, MacKenzie & Grayson,

So that someday, they may use the pillars I advance on the pages of this book in their own journey and become the next generation of champions for organizational culture.

With gratitude,

No author can go it alone. Someone who has a story to tell or wisdom to impart starts the process with random thoughts and disjointed composition. A crackerjack wordsmith is needed to turn their words into a readable form and make the words come alive with meaning and enjoyment for the audience. I found such a person in Denise Meschmar Suttle. She was kind in her criticisms and edits while making my words readable and valuable to the reader. She went to great lengths to maintain the integrity of my style. I'm eternally grateful.

Wm. Gary Grimmer, I affectionately refer to as the Professor, is a globally recognized thought leader in the tourism industry. Without his mentorship & friendship over the last 31 years, my journey would not have been as enjoyable, enlightening, and meaningful. I am indebted to him for his guidance and encouragement.

There was never a doubt that I wanted Goodrich Publishing to carry this book to the finish line. Their experience, organization processes, advice, and savvy in the crowded and competitive publishing space provided the confidence and value I was looking for and needed. Thank you!

FOREWORD

Dennis Campbell cut his corporate cultural teeth at Southwest Airlines. He absorbed his lessons well. I suspect he instinctively already knew much of what he learned by virtue of his inherent nature, whether he realized it at the time or not. In short, he was a willing, eager, joyful, and highly successful student.

In the 1980s, when Southwest Airlines joined an airline industry trade association in Washington, D.C. (more to keep an eye on competitors than to emulate them), I represented Southwest at meetings. There I observed the behaviors of some of the industry's leading executives, several of whom were famous and much admired for business acumen and force of will. They would loudly and confidently argue a position, demanding with much table-pounding that others follow. At future meetings, they would argue just as forcefully—except their position had changed 180 degrees. In contrast, I observed that Southwest's leaders' constant advocacy was based on core values that never changed. Recessions come and go. Tactics change. Values, if they are good, true, and constitute the core of your business philosophy, remain.

Corporate Culture is not a "flavor of the month." It is a belief system founded upon solid core values and the business principles derived therefrom. Dennis Campbell is a believer. Most readers of his succinct yet thorough volume likely will become believers too.

Campbell alludes in his Epilogue to the Great Pandemic of 2020, the results of which are not known as of this writing. When the business record of winners and losers is published, I will wager that many enterprises adopting Campbell's model will survive and even thrive. Those that don't, won't. The victors' triumph will not be due to luck, but because (to borrow Mr. Campbell's phrase), they were "unbeatable"—not by a competitor, not by a recession, not even by a new virus.

Ron Ricks
Vice Chairman
Board of Directors
Southwest Airlines Co.

INTRODUCTION

Growing up in Annapolis, Maryland, from age 5-15, I spent considerable time at the United States Naval Academy, courtesy of a childhood friend, David Smalley, Jr. David's father was the head basketball coach at the Academy. It was the Academy that I was exposed for the first time to a unique culture. But I didn't know its definition at the time.

In the years that followed, I became immersed in military-oriented cultures while attending military boarding school, serving in the US Army as an Army Criminal Investigator, and by working undercover on a Drug Suppression Team in Germany in the late 1970s. Upon reflection, these experiences became the foundation for my development of self-awareness, situational awareness, and curiosity about organizational culture as I transitioned to corporate America.

After my military career, I had the benefit of working at Southwest Airlines and studying under company culture icons, the late Herb Kelleher, Founder and Chairman Emeritus, and Colleen Barrett, President Emeritus. Moving forward, armed with the cultural pillars I prescribe to be absolute for an unbeatable company, I molded and implemented these principles to help turn around anemic organizations.

When asked when I was going to write a book to expand on my keynote talk about The Seven Pillars of a Winning and Unbeatable Company Culture, quite frankly, I had not considered it a priority. But recently, I've realized that when speaking to audiences, my delivery of substantive takeaways and stories was falling short. I needed to map out details on how to transform a company that has unique circumstances. Effective speaking is expected to be educational, entertaining, and engaging, but statistically, less than one percent of the audience goes home and takes any action.

A business coach can help individual companies, but there are thousands of small to large-cap businesses that can benefit from a pivot to emphasize culture versus strategies. So here I am, writing this book.

It is my ardent belief that this book, and the sharing of personally transformational stories and anecdotes, will lead you to success. It is directed to the current and future generations of leaders who, if they truly embrace the cultural principles and make them a priority, will find pathways to an unbeatable company and profits beyond their wildest imagination.

You will not be peppered with statistics or studies as you read your way through this book. I read some time ago that 80% of all statistics were made up anyhow! I am not an academic delivering a message based on management and leadership teachings.

Instead, you will get my lens of experiences, opinions, and lessons as I lived them. I now share with you, in the most articulate and straightforward form I can muster, The Seven Pillars of a Winning and Unbeatable Culture that correspond with the seven letters of the word- CULTURE. Enjoy.

THE 1ST PILLAR

Commit to Hiring for Attitude. Period!

In the 1960s and well into the 1970s, newly appointed CEOs generally rose from the ranks of the finance and accounting departments. Very few were selected from the sales or marketing track for the C-suite. By the 1980s, the competitive landscape began to pressure company market share, combined with the evolution of advertising and promotion options. Now, the sales and marketing professionals became the favorite "go-to" people for leading a company.

Concurrent to this trend, personnel departments were rebranded as human resources. In some companies, well into the 2000s, they became known as the people department. However well-intentioned, many of these people departments were in name only, and little was understood about measuring the importance of company culture. Mind you, the human resources star was rising, and CEOs became more dependent on their human resource executives for advice, training curricula, labor law, and for keeping the company out of court for a myriad of employment-based lawsuits.

The human resources professional is today's top advisor to CEOs and other C-Suite executives, as well as directors and managerial-level leaders for matters of employment law, counseling, training, recognition programs, and recruiting. Candidly, their role encompasses areas vital to setting the tone for workforce happiness, safety, and productivity. The most important of which, arguably, is recruiting.

Yet, there is a fly in the ointment: application and recruitment web-based platforms. While this technology is impressively capable of collecting tens of thousands of resumes and job applications, thus efficient for the process of recruiting, they are dangerously flawed.

Today, we have the pervasive practice of high-volume application platforms that use keywords associated with education, experience, certifications, etc. These platforms filter resumes and applicants to a shortlist for a phone interview, then filter more to an in-person interview with a group or a hiring manager. The entire process is focused on the candidate's background, education, and certifications.

Mis-hires have a dotted line tracing back to the algorithms of bots and spiders which filter and capture a shortlist of applicants using keywords like MBA, Bachelors, certifications, project manager, director, sales metrics, industry, and the list goes on. The applicants may be phone screened before in-person interviews. In virtually all cases, the interview templates and the recruitment platforms emphasize describing past employment experiences and accomplishments, educational majors, size/scope of the past budget, and project responsibilities.

While technology has refined the hiring process, it flies in the face of the 1st Pillar for creating an unbeatable company culture. Minimal emphasis is placed on personal attitudes toward working with others across departmental lines, volunteering to pitch in when it is not their job, or basic human interaction. Translation: grace, gratitude, and service.

This system flaw is dangerous in the sense that mis-hires will eventually be recognized by others in the employee group as a wrong fit. This can affect the group's level of enthusiasm for their work, resulting in unproductive energy and time spent wondering how and why management could have hired this person. Simultaneously, the culture of the organization becomes stagnant, or worse, erodes into "why should I care?"

Even Myers-Briggs®, DiSC®, and other personality assessment tools fall short of getting to the essence of a person's character traits on the subject of service to others. When a person is naturally attuned to be of service, he or she is willing to help anybody with any project or challenge, within the team, with other teams, and most importantly, for the customer.

Hiring for attitude can reduce your mis-hires and turnover rate tremendously, although it may not appear on the profit and loss statement. Your human resources folks can record metrics on this for you and should. This is the foundational secret sauce in building an unbeatable culture.

To be clear, I have made hiring mistakes. You will make hiring mistakes. The key is to minimize those mistakes by keeping the recruitment focus on attitude, first and foremost. When a bad fit or attitude deficiency is identified, take immediate action without delaying out of the fear that you will be viewed as having failed in the hiring decision.

If termination is the only solution, be certain it is conducted with LUV*; the same measure of LUV you would exhibit with a cherished employee (more on this in the 3rd Pillar). This, too, is a part of a winning culture and will be recognized and respected.

Hiring for attitude is not just for entry-level or hourly employees. It should be the primary criterion at all levels of hiring, including the C-Suite. Corporate America's history is rife with once-great companies that eventually failed, such as Braniff Airlines, Levitz Furniture, and Toys' R Us. There must be a reason connected to culture (hiring for attitude) that caused certain companies to fail and others in their space to survive and even thrive.

As an example from my Southwest days, when an airline hires pilots, applicants are expected to be qualified with specific flight certifications and pilot-in-command hours in a jet. But candidates make the shortlist based on observable traits, such as helpfulness, generosity of spirit, and humility.

Which candidates exhibit a willingness to help passengers using wheelchairs down the jetway and assist them into a seat? Which candidates are willing to help flight attendants reset the seatbelts before passengers start boarding a new flight? Consider attitude first, then look at the required professional qualifications to make the hiring decision.

When I was recruited by Gary Grimmer away from Southwest Airlines in 1989 to be the vice president of convention sales and marketing for the Albuquerque Convention and Visitors Bureau (now Visit Albuquerque), I had never worked in direct hotel sales or a destination marketing organization (DMO). People with experience in those businesses were the usual pool for recruitment.

With a staff exhibiting anemic sales performance and low morale, it was risky for Gary to look outside this traditional field. He knew me as a board member for Visit Albuquerque, as the territory marketing and sales executive for Southwest, and perhaps my reputation, but that was it. When he invited me to lunch with the board chairman, Tom Chase, I thought they were going to put the squeeze on me for chairing a committee.

My background was purely airline operations, marketing, and criminal investigations. I learned later, however, that he had hired me for attitude first and foremost, and then my marketing skills acquired at Southwest Airlines. It seems he had observed me in two areas connected to attitude: a.) Southwest Airlines was a disruptor in commercial aviation; their processes were different from competitors in regard to passenger seating, luggage transfers, and interaction with travel agents. In short, this was not an easy sell in the emerging markets. Gary thought, if this guy has the attitude to persuade and convert the travel agents and business travelers, he can sell Albuquerque, a destination that is unique in its own right. b.) Gary had observed me as a board member in dealing with the contentious matter of using federal grant funds (UDAG) to subsidize the development of a new downtown hotel. There were strong opinions on the matter that sparked heated debate, causing a fracture in the relationships among the hotel community and with some elected officials. I supported the sorely needed hotel development, as did the board. I lent a hand with the measured diplomacy and conversations about why the additional room inventory would benefit the entire community. This board activity occurred at least two years before Gary recruited me for the VP role.

So, what are the actionable takeaways here? Begin by establishing a set of recruitment questions that peels the layers back to reveal the applicants' views on service to others. Do they volunteer their time at soup kitchens, a charitable cause, their place of worship? Why do they do it? Do they genuinely wish to make a difference in people's lives? Do they view it as giving back, or seeking recognition?

Get these questions and follow-up dialogue into the technology platforms, phone screening, and in-person interview processes. Set ALL experience, education, and certifications to the side. Once you have a shortlist of candidates based on what you feel is the right attitude, then start to examine the background, accomplishments, and other specifics related to the position for making a final decision on the best candidate.

During my keynote talk, I share a photo of the parking lot at my local Fry's Grocery store. The photo depicts two shopping carts that were not returned to the cart corral by the customers. One is taking up a single parking space 10 feet from the corral, and the other is about 15 feet from the corral, taking up space in the corners of four parking spaces. It takes real effort to park a shopping cart in such a way that it impedes parking in four spaces. You do not want to hire that person.

It is up to you to develop questions in the hiring process and application platforms that help you learn if a particular candidate is someone who returns their cart to the corral or not.

THE 2ND PILLAR
Undertake Organizational Evangelism

I used the word "evangelism" on purpose, both for a bit of shock value, but to also describe the level of discernible commitment to the cause or causes of the company. To be clear, I am not referring to cult-like commitment. Some companies have been labeled as a cult and I view the definition of a cult as a unilateral model. Followers (employees) are expected to behave a certain way, execute the plan without question, and accept the principal demands. There is no room or opportunity for individualism or input.

This was very apparent in a particular international hotel company of which I am familiar. The core middle management and senior management team did not socialize outside of their company peers and colleagues, nor did they seek substantive input from line employees. Now, in their defense, they were making a statement to the public about their brand with this approach, but formality and stiffness carried deeper, and in my opinion, held this company back from greatness.

Today, they are not one of the top four hotel companies globally. I observed tremendous employee turnover at this company in the 1980s through the early 2000s. This culture model, at that time, was rooted in a unilateral philosophy from the top. To their credit, since the mid-2000s, this company has become more employee-centric in its culture.

Alternatively, Southwest Airlines may have a uniquely relaxed branding approach as experienced by the public and by comparison to other airlines. Yet they carry and advocate this relaxed and inclusive philosophy throughout their internal systems, not just for branding and public consumption. The employee group is encouraged to make suggestions, challenge the prevailing practices, and participate in virtually every operational decision process.

It would be very easy when contemplating uniform changes for flight attendants and airport personnel, mechanics, and so forth, for senior management to send out RFPs to vendors, have them respond, make a decision, announce the decision to the employees, and roll out the new uniforms. However, Southwest goes to great lengths to have the employees who will be wearing the uniforms be part of the committee (HR, marketing, in-flight, maintenance, etc.) and participate in this decision. Their input and opinions matter. The line employees are participants in scores of such committees at Southwest, and the resulting feeling is one of mutual respect between management and employees.

In 1985 Southwest failed to increase its net profit over the prior year*. This affected that year's employee profit-sharing to be less than the year prior. It caused senior management, like in any company, to examine where expenses could be reduced as they continued to also plan for growing topline revenue. Commonly, company practices would be to convene the senior management team, have every department head propose budget cuts, and eventually create a plan for implementation.

Not so at Southwest Airlines, which for the record, was at that time and is today, the most expense efficient airline in the industry. What did they do? They went to the employees. They developed a contest whereby employees formed teams of 4-8 employees for submitting expense reduction ideas for consideration. If, after review and research of the suggestion, complete with metrics narrative, the company implemented the idea, that team would get points equal to the first-year savings from the adopted idea. The team then redeemed points from a catalog facilitated through Maritz Incentive House. One of our team's ideas was adopted and gave us so many points that I was able to furnish my entire house with Thomasville furniture. True story.

As I recall, by the time the program concluded, the company implemented over $100 million in saving ideas derived from employee input. This is a prima facie example of a component in developing real corporate evangelism through employee participation and sharing, up and down the organization chart.

Zillow, the real estate listings and research data platform, calls it turning the lights on.* In other words, share everything with your employees, including the financials. It does not matter that you are a family-owned, privately-held business. If you want to insulate your company from competitive forces taking your customers, from extinction in the wake of economic speed bumps, or from other unforeseen roadblocks, *"Turn the Lights On."*

At Zillow, their employee comforts rank with those you would expect at tech giants like Google and Facebook. If an employee wants a shade for their cubicle's fluorescent lighting, an ergonomic chair, or a standing desk for variable work heights, Zillow provides it. Their break room is like a small organic grocery store with fruits, trail mix, and more. I could write a whole page on the other benefits in medical, 401K matches, and stock gifts. Zillow has cracked the code for understanding the importance of the work-family happiness, reducing turnover, and ensuring Positively Outrageous Service* to buyers and real estate professionals in the local market.

The concept of corporate evangelism needs to be rooted in a sustainable buy-in to a cause, a series of tactical plans and reinforced continually. It is the exact opposite of the idea of "drinking the Kool-Aid," which is blind allegiance to a cult-like ideology. A motivating fiery speech by the CEO might get the group fired up in the short term, but that enthusiasm will eventually burn out. A planned program to include employees in building the organization, with tangible rewards along the way, will help your company on its way to true evangelism.

The Hell's Angels understand organization evangelism and exude such through their clothing, pledge of loyalty, iconic mode of transportation, and causes. I don't pretend to know their causes or variations by chapter, but I know they exist.

Too often, organization executives will confuse the mission with causes. True evangelism is born from causes and a string of other fundamentals, not the mission.

At Southwest Airlines, the original *mission* was to provide air transportation between Dallas, Houston, and San Antonio, converting business travelers who would otherwise drive to those cities. The business model was to provide this transportation in a fun manner for customers and employees, at an affordable price, and with a frequency that provided convenient options for customers to do business and still be home for dinner.

The *cause* was to build a work-family that focused on employee individualism, participation in company decisions, and rewards, not just in salary, but in the financial success of the company.

True healthy corporate evangelism is the path to repelling competitive forces and will serve as your leadership legacy. Where do you start? First, the company should have a historian responsible for collecting any material, products, tangible projects, or photos. These can be displayed throughout the common areas so that new and existing employees are frequently passing by these mementos and occasionally stop to review.

This person or committee is usually from the human resources department. Former employees, executives, vendors, all should be contacted for what they might have in their possession that can help reconstruct the chronological story. This piece helps elevate evangelism through a sense of belonging to something bigger than just a job.

We are not just talking about the CEO on magazine covers or awards from the Chamber of Commerce. Do not make it an "I Love Me Wall" for the CEO or other C-suite executives. Save that for their personal office space.

We are really talking about capturing significant events, products, and equipment milestones of the company. If you ever visit Apple or Southwest Airlines headquarters, you will see displays of their first products, clothing, and uniform styles, up to the present day, a chronology of corporate evolution.

If you are an executive who does not want the previous owner's or leaderships' history displayed or memorialized, then I submit to you a.) you are not truly committed to achieving an unbeatable company, and b.) you and your company are unlikely to achieve legacy status and are likely vulnerable to competitive forces. Companies I have advised have recognized the impact these historical displays have on employees, connecting them with the magnitude of accomplishments that they are now a part of.

How do you know you are making progress toward healthy evangelism? There may be subtle signs or perhaps a big breakthrough sign. As a consultant in this area, it is my responsibility to help observe and report on these for a client's company.

I can share my own "aha!" moment during my tenure at Visit Albuquerque. Not long after I arrived, I wanted a moniker or nickname for the team. I observed a lack of confidence among the team members, and they did not seem to feel that they belonged to a strong work-family.

I chose to name our team the A-Team. This was partly after the popular 1980s television show starring George Peppard and Mr. T in quasi-military special forces, and partly because Albuquerque begins with an A. I thought this name could inspire the group to be an unbeatable sales force with the pride of belonging to an elite group.

Not long after we launched our moniker, a hotel general manager delivered a cocktail napkin with the colorized photo impression of the A-Team television stars to my office. This was my first indication that peers and stakeholders were taking notice and approved. I immediately had the napkin matted, framed, and hung in the hallway of our offices.

A few years later, I received a call from the sales director at another hotel in Albuquerque. She said that Mr. T was in the hotel. I asked if she thought he would sign our napkin, and the response was, yes, in exchange for a bottle of Dom Perignon champagne delivered to his room. I agreed and paid for the champagne. The napkin got signed and displayed in our offices. The team was ecstatic, and I knew then that we were indeed achieving an unbeatable culture, with the added benefit of admiration from our stakeholders.

Our A-Team moniker even got the attention of City Hall. Even when I was graciously honored in 1996 by then Albuquerque Mayor Martin Chavez with an executive ordered namesake day, the citation referred to OUR A-Team as feared and respected by our competitors. Those words were of enormous joy for me, more so, even than the executive order itself. Not to be braggadocious, but I mention it here for validation of the point.

I recommend establishing a nickname for your team or business unit. Conduct a contest among the team to come up with the name. Then each year, establish a mantra. This is a call to action for the team to rally around. I remember one year the mantra for our sales and services team was "Take No Prisoners," then after achieving record sales, the next year was "And Then Some." It may sound a little hokey on the pages of this book, but employees LUV a good team moniker and goal-connected mantra.

As a leader of a legacy company, continue to reconstruct lost history and build upon it by memorializing new milestones in products, equipment, and notable events during your tenure. If yours is a recent startup, capture your successes and evolution often with video, photos, and objects. Some of the photos, film, and office objects I observed in the Amazon documentary about Jeff Bezos dating back to the start in his garage were fantastic.

For me, the definition of evangelism outside of theology is winning the hearts of those on my team, instilling in them a sense of belonging to a work-family, and delivering a feeling they are part of a crusade for something much more significant than just a job. In the end, there are myriad creative ways to win their hearts, and countless ideas to create meaningful causes.

The big brother to success sharing is profit sharing. This does not mean it has to be in the form of stock, just participation in the net profit. Employees who are given a stake in the financial success of the company have proven in hundreds of such companies that they are more conscientious with raw materials waste, industrial accident reductions, customer service, and retention, and the list goes on.

Additionally, they will school and police their peers if they observe someone wasting resources or being reckless in their work activities. I remember at Southwest Airlines, senior ramp agents (those that load the luggage into the belly of the aircraft, among other tasks) would observe a new "ramper" grab a customer suitcase or garment bag by the handle and throw it onto the belt-loader that moves luggage up to the person stacking in the belly. That new ramper got a spirited briefing on how broken handles and damaged luggage claims affect profit sharing and the company reputation for service. No leadership counseling was necessary.

I took the cost/expense saving experience at Southwest with me to Visit Albuquerque in February 1989. This company was nine years old at the time, a not-for-profit marketing association that broke away from the Greater Albuquerque Chamber of Commerce in 1980. While you cannot offer profit sharing in a not-for-profit company, I implemented a success sharing plan in the first year, separate from the sales performance bonuses. Every dollar saved in the expense line items as compared to the prior year was shared with the employees on a 50/50 basis. The company benefited, placing its share of the savings back into sales and marketing programs, and the employees enjoyed their fifty percent share in the form of cash.

Give profit-sharing priority consideration in transforming your company and its culture. Let me add, you will be surprised -- no, shocked -- at how much more net profit you will realize if evangelism is implemented. Meanwhile, competitors will be lagging behind you in good times and failing to survive during turbulent times.

THE 3RD PILLAR

Leading with LUV*

This phrase is borrowed from the title of the book written in 2010 by Ken Blanchard and Colleen Barrett.* Colleen is President Emeritus of Southwest Airlines and a distance mentor, and Blanchard, of course, is the famed author of *The One Minute Manager*© and many other leadership books. The "LUV" spelling comes from the Wall Street ticker symbol for Southwest Airlines stock.

When you become responsible for the performance and wellbeing of another person or a group of persons, you have now become a leader in position, if not also in title. Colleen put it best in her book, "Anytime you seek to influence the thinking, behavior, or development of people in their personal or professional life, you are taking on the role of a leader."*

Translation: you now have responsibility for a new family's wellbeing and development, your work-family. Sure, you may think the only family you have is your biological family, or adopted family, extended family, place of worship family, and so forth. *Au contraire.* Once you have accepted a role in the workplace to lead the performance metrics of one or more people, you now have another family.

Company leaders at all levels profess to place a priority on employees with recognition, rewards, morale booster events, and such. They are not paying lip service to this; they genuinely believe it. Many have been to leadership training and seminars, read self-improvement books, and perhaps, if lucky, had a mentor or two along the way. But their "all-in" core commitment often falls short of truly leading the work family with LUV.

My training and experiences in the United States Army and exposure to leadership principles, albeit from a lower enlisted perspective, advances the theme of the mission (winning wars) running parallel with the health and wellbeing of the troops. However, the mission is often slightly or acutely ahead of troop welfare as a priority.

Just read about some of the famous generals of the 20th Century and how hard they pushed troops in the name of mission first. General George S. Patton comes to mind. Why is that? In warfare, it is truly life and death circumstances that necessitate training and hardships. When you are short of supplies, in adverse conditions and outnumbered, out resourced and scared, you can adapt and persevere to save the life of the soldier, sailor, marine, airman or coastie fighting next to you and win wars. Harsh training methods that have been the legend of veterans' storytelling are designed to build a sense of rarified cohesion to execute orders without questioning. This is a form of corporate mantra that has been referred to as *esprit de corps*, or in other words, organizational evangelism.

In the corporate world, there are also wars: competitive wars and wars against unforeseen speedbumps (raw material expense hikes, economic recessions). If the employee group is not the highest priority, they may not have the enthusiasm or motivation to rise to the task of hurdling the challenges lying before your company. Let us not forget, you cannot just quit when you do not like something about your role in the military, but you can in a civilian job. Employees must feel connected to a higher purpose.

Working at Southwest Airlines initially in airport operations and specifically, the customer service supervisor role, I was immediately impressed by how well the ticket counter and gate (customer service) staff functioned. We were thoroughly trained, everybody was conscious of resources used or wasted, and we had fun.

These airport customer service jobs are not easy, often filled with repetitive questions from customers (where is my gate, where's the restroom, why is my flight delayed, why don't I have a seat?). In short, these employees are on the front lines of the customer interface, just like flight attendants and reservation personnel. Airline operations is a well-choreographed dance in ideal conditions, but processes in place through "POS - Positively Outrageous Service"* in the face of often harsh impatience and demands by customers, can be quite draining of positive energy.

I was mission-driven and trained, so this notion of enormous focus on taking outstanding care of employees, and they will handle taking care of the customers with grace and enthusiasm and POS, was new to me. As the late Herb Kelleher would often share in speeches, interviews, and quarterly updates to Wall Street analysts, "Treat your employees like family, they will, in turn, treat customers like family, and the profits will follow and take care of the shareholders."*

Today, there is a cult-like following of Southwest customers, despite not having assigned seats, a first-class section, and other such on-board amenities as other airlines. Yet, Southwest is the largest domestic carrier in terms of domestic flight operations and passenger boardings.

It may interest you to know, as of this writing, Southwest Airlines has never laid off or furloughed an employee, failed to make a net profit in any quarter in any year since the first quarter of operations in 1971. No other airlines can make the same claim. Southwest has consistently ranked in the top four airlines for customer satisfaction, on-time performance, and fewest bags lost/damaged as measured by the U.S. Department of Transportation. *

"So what?" you might say. Southwest was a one-off anomaly that started as a company that offered a profit-sharing plan, that hired for attitude, and had a mission of providing a high frequency of flights scheduled to three destinations, low fares, and fun - the three "f's." Yes, all true, except that it is not a one-off anomaly. I personally took the principles that I learned at Southwest (including leading with LUV) with me to a future, and much more senior, leadership role when I inherited a work-family.

As I shared in The 1st Pillar, in 1989, the CEO of Visit Albuquerque was looking for a new vice president of sales and marketing for the convention sales division. The city was expanding the convention center by more than 100,000 square feet, and there was a new 395-room hotel development coming out of the ground at the same time.

Only one future convention had been booked for this new inventory. I was being recruited to turn this around. The team had low morale from falling short of their goals and endured significant scrutiny and criticism from the stakeholders that depended upon Visit Albuquerque for a substantial share of their business leads. The convention bid process required a great deal of collaboration among the stakeholders, including hotels, attractions, event venues, suppliers, and the like.

Immediately, I set about implementing The Seven Pillars of a Winning Culture. I created several perks and programs for achieving corporate evangelism. For example, I used my reserved parking space for the employee of the month (I never used the parking space during my entire seven-year tenure). Members of the team were openly boasting about how they were going to get the parking space next month. I never realized how powerful that perk could be in developing the team culture.

I had a cartoon sticker program. If you collected enough goofy cartoon stickers earned from customers' letters of praise about you, then you received a dinner for two at a very nice restaurant. We established a quarterly competition among the sales managers to score points for various sales activities, with the top scorer rewarded with a plaque and honors at a quarterly sales team dinner.

The team got complete access and briefings on the meaning of the financial P & L and had the green light to challenge any views or opinions of mine and others respectfully. I regularly checked on their family's well-being, brought each employee a small souvenir from any vacation I took, gave each team member a small holiday gift made by local artists, rewarded them with success sharing funds for saving the company money in key line items, and right down the list of seven pillars.

What other promises did I make, and what performance did I expect? I promised to be involved in every bid they wanted me involved in, at any level they wanted. I met with them individually to determine what they felt was going right and what they thought was not going so well. In essence, I was doing what Herb Kelleher said about his successor, Colleen Barrett:

she knows how to love people to success. That is what I was attempting to demonstrate: a genuine love for my work-family that I was asking so much of in return.

If you have not already added *In Search of Excellence* by Tom Peters to your business bookshelf, do it. His concept of "management by walking around (MBWA)" leads to my next takeaway. Get out of your office, circulate with the employees routinely, shoulder to shoulder. Do this not by announcing it or scheduling it a week or months in advance. Make it spontaneous. Do not treat it as a tour of their work area. They will get a kick out of it, and their immediate supervisors or directors will be on edge, which the rank and file also most likely enjoy.

Show them you can do some heavy lifting and get your hands dirty. Drive the forklift, unload a pallet, go on a sales call with one of your team members, and extend this involvement to all levels and classifications of employees. Ask questions. Start with relationship questions about how their family is doing. What are some of their hobbies, music interests, where did they grow up?

Then you can evolve the conversation into questions about their specific role at the company. How many cans do we get in a pallet? How much does an entire pallet of product weigh? What is the hardest part of this job? What drives you crazy about some of the processes (think about the TV show *Undercover Boss*). How can it be done easier and smarter in your view? How could we modify the maintenance schedule of our vehicles that would make them last longer, lowering the quarterly expense?

Then, if their suggestions are implemented, reward them, as suggested in The 2nd Pillar. This connects you deeper to them as a human who happens to be in a leadership role and further solidifies the quest for an unbeatable culture.

Two notes of caution here: if you ask for suggestions and ideas casually in the field (and you should), make sure these are researched with an unbiased lens, and not forgotten. If it is not feasible for any reason the research revealed, make sure you explain it to the employee who made the suggestion. Do this personally. It will enhance your credibility and the health of your work-family culture. If you do not, your credibility will be eroded with that employee and likely his/her peers, which in turn will erode progress you were making in achieving corporate evangelism.

Secondly, your direct reports need to know that you don't think less of them because one of their employees came up with an idea and they didn't, or that they should somehow feel threatened. They should embrace the idea, research it, and, if implemented, shine the light on that employee. As the leader, you will be viewed as developing your team effectively, embracing creativity, and fully participating in the cause.

You may lose a few people along the way. Leading with LUV is not just about easy-going, lenient management style, or being liked. It sometimes requires tough love. But discipline or termination should never be a surprise to someone. There should have been multiple and ample conversations about course-correcting behavior and attitude concerns and the ultimate question of "are you the right fit for this team?"

If a person is not the right fit, letting the matter linger and doing nothing will affect the attitude and morale of the entire group and will erode your credibility as a leader. Do not ignore this difficult responsibility. It can tear apart everything you have been working so hard to build. When a termination is necessary, do a self-evaluation of why it happened. Where did you fail this person? Wrong fit? More one-on-one course correction time? Was there another role in the company more suitable as an alternative to termination? In other words, how do you guard against repeating this failure?

I will circle back to how our convention sales team reacted to these new practices. From 1989 to 1996, the team contracted more than 1.15M room nights in future conference business (one hotel room for one night = one room night). Four of the seven years of my tenure were record bookings (more than 200,000 room nights each year), half of which was business destined for the convention center.

The hotels and other stakeholders became big supporters as we delivered better quality bid leads, polished our convention services deliverables, proactively worked to close business at higher ratios, and demonstrated how much we cared about hosting a particular client event. The energy I poured into caring for the A-Team was, in turn, poured into their performance for closing deals and providing Positively Outrageous Service for convention and events.

Did we have strategies in our bids? Of course. But our culture oozed from the pores of the team, and it was felt by the conference organizers. During those years, we were outspent in promotional/advertising weight by as much as 3-5:1 by our primary regional competition (Phoenix, Salt Lake, San Diego, San Antonio, Tucson, and a few others).

I am not perfect at always leading with LUV. I have had my share of missteps, but I have learned from those, grown, and remembered the poor decision when faced with a similar situation. You must always ask yourself, am I leading with LUV in this matter? Today I ask myself, what would Herb and Colleen do in this situation? It prevents me from leaping into, and drowning in, poor leadership decisions. One such decision that comes to mind is when I took a client account away from a sales manager.

The situation was in a delicate phase of negotiations. The client had signaled they were prepared to cancel their commitment to our destination, and my skepticism kicked in about this being a possible ploy to get deeper concessions from us.

With the dynamics of this ongoing negotiation being complicated, I did not do what would have been in the best interest of my employee: talk it through, advise, counsel, and empower her to continue working to salvage the account. Instead, I panicked and took the heavy-handed route. It is a decision I regret to this day.

Taking the account from her was sending a terrible message of mistrust, which evolved into a fractured relationship and was not unnoticed by my other direct reports. This had implications for the organization's culture.

What should I have done differently? Talked it through, sought more in-depth feedback on what she knew about the account, and advised her to guard against any semblance of our passive acquiescence on the client's actions.

Earlier in this chapter I mentioned that I would encourage anyone on the team, direct reports, or otherwise, to challenge any views or opinions. I want to address the practice of being present when in a meeting with one or several of your work family. There are leadership books and seminars that include being present as part of a genuine demonstration that you care.

I had a habit early in my leadership roles of multi-tasking for efficiency. I was young, full of energy, and maximizing my productivity, based on my way of thinking. This was before smartphones with texting, emails on our phone, and, heaven forbid, a Facebook or LinkedIn alert you just cannot wait to check. I would go from an email on desktop and a letter in draft, to a file folder my executive assistant had for must-reads and another folder with documents requiring my signature.

One day, I was engaged in multi-tasking while one of my sales managers was giving a briefing on a bid and seeking my feedback on strategy and next steps. Suddenly, she says, "DC! Are you listening to me?" My thought bubble was, "of course I'm listening to you. I can do several tasks at once and listen to your briefing!" Well, maybe I can. That is not the point.

The message I was sending is that whatever is important enough for them to talk about is not important enough to deserve my undivided attention. This was a tough habit for me to break. In this case, I pled guilty, came out from behind my desk, and sat in the chair next to her.

Sitting side-by-side became my new practice and habit to prevent me from doing it again. I made sure to move to a chair next to the person I was meeting with so that I was truly present. Whether it is for a scheduled or impromptu meeting, once they are invited in, you need to be present. These days, if you don't know that people hate it when you check text messages or email during a meeting or conversation, you likely need more self-awareness and a practice that will help you to truly be present.

THE 4TH PILLAR
Training, Training, Training

As a staunch advocate of training, I am astonished at how many companies, when under budget pressures, will cut training first. Many leaders look to the training budget for cuts to shore up the revenue vs. expense forecast or a misstep midyear in an expense category. They just make it up by shifting funds from the training budget.

Some, I have found during my business consulting, do not even have training in their budget forecast plans for the next fiscal year. They are just winging it when a training opportunity is requested or presents itself. Depending upon the mood the decision-maker or the financial health of the organization at the time, you either get to attend the training; or not.

I will cut advertising before I cut training. It is not only crucial for the development of the individual and their skills; it reinforces the message that you care enough to invest in your employees.

There is an old joke among company leaders: "The CFO says to the CEO, what if we train them and they leave?" The CEO retorts, "What if we don't train them and they stay?" This humorous exchange should alarm leaders at all levels.

In the airline sector, many federal regulations require mandatory training at various calendar benchmarks for pilots, flight attendants, mechanics, and others. Yet at every level up and down the organizational chart, there was always training not mandated by the government.

I can remember when I was in the airport operations role. We had regular customer service seminars for understanding true service delivery in tough and stressful situations. We also had one on how to handle a major incident, like a hijacking, learning whose authority took precedence, and what our roles were. Marketers were trained not only in sales techniques but also in handling the media following an incident. Of course, I had reason to appreciate and almost expect the training, since, in the Army, there was plenty of it, all mandatory!

When I arrived at Visit Albuquerque, it was the middle of the fiscal year, and I was shocked to learn that there was no training budgeted for the sales team or the administrative assistants. No one had ever attended any formalized training since their arrival at the company. No wonder we were being outfoxed by the competition on bids! Sending someone to exhibit at a tradeshow booth does not constitute training.

It was up to me to be creative because we needed training, and we needed it now. I decided not to move budgets around in different categories until I was comfortable that I understood the implications. So, until the end of the fiscal year (five months away), I needed a creative approach to offer training.

I turned to books and movies. Self-improvement books, as well as movies with strong themes or social messages, were just the ticket. I researched then selected titles that fit the training I wanted to focus on. Initially, the focus was to be on selling, teamwork, servant's purpose, and HR friendly: *The Art of War* (Sun Tzu, 5th Century BCE), *Shawshank Redemption* (Warner Bros., 1994), *The Sound Of Music* (20th Century Fox, 1965), *The 7 Habits of Highly Effective People* (Stephen R. Covey, 1989), and in later years newer movies like *Seabiscuit* (Universal, 2003) and books like *The Five Dysfunctions of a Team* (Patrick Lencioni, 2002).

I assigned folks into teams of two. They collaborated on a briefing paper, presented to me, on what they learned from the book or movie that had a direct correlation to their job. Then at some point, I would have each twosome share their paper with the entire team.

The exercise creates a wonderful exchange of ideas and learnings. I continued to use books and movies as training tools while later adding traditional outside training for all personnel. It truly is food for the work soul. Sir Richard Branson is quoted as saying, "Train people well enough so they can leave, treat them well enough, so they don't want to." This is brilliant. I will never compromise on a training budget or advise a client to compromise. I will recommend that the advertising budget be reduced before the training budget.

A lesser utilized training tool is job shadowing, ride alongs, or formal mentoring. If you have a direct report, or an employee two levels below you, shadow you, you are getting a twofer. First, you are leading with LUV by acknowledging their value, and second, they are getting real exposure to what you do daily.

This can lead to preparing for a future leadership role or simply a better understanding of how their current role fits in the bigger picture. A more formal mentorship program establishes a set of goals, deadlines for specific deliverables for both you as a mentor and the mentee. I find this tool highly underrated for its purpose and impact, and not implemented as widely as you would think. If I were a CEO today, I would recommend all managers and supervisors have two mentees each.

Actor Denzel Washington said in his book, *A Hand to Guide Me* (2006) "At the end of the day, it's not about what you have or even what you've accomplished. It's about what you've done with those accomplishments. It's about who you've lifted up, who you've made better. It's about what you've given back."

Mentorship should not be a burden; it should be automatic, mandatory, and given with enthusiasm.

THE 5TH PILLAR
Use Humor and Humility

Not everybody is capable of being funny. Some think they are funny, but they are not. If you are one of these, then focus on humility. I remember when I had my first one-on-one alone time with Herb Kelleher sometime in late 1983 or early 1984. I was picking him up at the El Paso airport and taking him to a Chamber of Commerce luncheon, where he was the featured speaker.

I had been with Southwest Airlines less than a year and was only three-plus years out of military service. I had just purchased a brand-new Mazda RX 7, Ferrari red. He climbed in and, after firing up his trademark cigarette, said to me, "Dang, nice car. How much are we paying you?"

Now, he was joking, because he had to know, plus or minus, what my pay range was. He was humorously paying me a backhanded compliment. He went on to ask, "Do you play golf?" "Not much," I replied, "only when it's necessary for business."

"What's your handicap?" he continued. "I don't think I have one officially, but usually score 18-20 over par," I answered. "Good," he said. "I don't trust any executive that is below a 10 handicap; they're not working hard enough." At this, we both had a great laugh.

He was saying, if you read between the lines, that he was committed to one cause, and that was Southwest Airlines. He was not the stereotypical CEO who is spending time on hobbies like golf. It was a validation of the cause I signed up for, not just a job, and he put me at ease with the conversation.

Herb was great at both humor and humility. He was asked from time to time how he, as a lawyer and founder of the company, became its CEO. His answer was always the same: Because he was not sufficiently qualified for any other roles at the company.

That is brilliant humility. I am only occasionally funny, but I have learned to use humor in the form of self-deprecation to allow direct reports and line employees to get a sense that I am genuinely approachable. When your employees are comfortable making fun of you, you are on the right track for cementing trust in the relationship.

On at least two occasions that I can recall from my time at Visit Albuquerque, both humor and humility came into play. The first occasion, the team had indicated that they wanted to participate in the American Cancer Society "Relay for Life®" cancer walk. It was a 24-hour continuous walk commitment. I thought it was a great cause, and more importantly, the team was united in their desire to execute the plan together.

I either offered or agreed when asked to dress like Klinger from the TV show *Mash* and stay with them for the entire relay. Someone found a beautiful long formal dress and long formal gloves and a boa that I wore to cheer the team on. It was a great bonding experience for the team, but I cannot lay any claim to brilliance. I remembered Herb Kelleher wore the Klinger dress and ensemble to a company holiday party one year. It was a huge success and validation of his willingness to be silly when the occasion arose.

As to the second occasion, I loved finely tailored men's clothing and kept up with styles of the day. I think I acquired this penchant from the precision tailoring of the Army dress blues uniform. At one point in my military career, I was a uniformed Military Policeman, with additional duties for the US Army Europe Honor Guard, specifically the Color Guard team.

Fast forward to the late '80s and '90s; I went through a phase of wearing custom made French cuffed shirts with my initials monogrammed on the cuff. One birthday, the staff was kind enough to recognize it, and a sales manager even made and wore mock-up French cuffs made from paper. We all got a big laugh at the joke and creativity. It was great fun, but what I liked best was that she was comfortable enough to poke fun at the boss. I hope my former direct reports would concur with that assessment.

If your associates do not see you as funny or humble, it may be because you are stuck in pride mode. Pride is the Achilles heel of human behavior, holding us back from a true servant's heart. The opposite virtue is humility. According to theologians, the essential vice, the utmost evil, is pride.

Unchastity, anger, greed, drunkenness, and other vices are mere fleabites in comparison. This is paraphrasing a quote from famed author C.S. Lewis. Think about that. Anger, greed, and drunkenness are "mere fleabites" compared to pride and the damage it can cause to yourself and others.

As a leader, you should be aware that employees are automatically apprehensive about engagement with you. Help your team feel it is OK to make fun of the boss, even the CEO, in a respectful manner. We tease our friends and family from time to time, so it should be with your work-family. Use your time in the field, interacting with them to display your humor and humility and do it regularly. You will be pleasantly surprised at how much you will enjoy it. Setting pride aside clears a broad path for humility and humor to do the bonding.

THE 6TH PILLAR
Release Control for Decisions

Leaders in business, government, and even religious faiths, often exhibit the strong behaviors that we label as Type A or High D. In an office, that drive and ambition needs to be harnessed. Unbridled, it is like a bull in a china shop, breaking everything in its path, including good people and optimal culture. Yes, the DiSC® test and the Myers-Briggs® test can help you understand your level of unconscious controlling behavior, and help you move toward greater self-awareness.

I want to encourage you to look at this a bit differently. If you require all decisions to go through you, then you are not fostering a culture that has the agility, energy, and total motivation factor, or ToMo* (concept created by Lindsay McGregor and Neel Doshi) that will allow your company to navigate turbulent waters.

You are placing the company at risk of extinction or being eclipsed by one of your competitors. Furthermore, if you maintain control of essential programming decisions, you are not lifting and developing the next generation of leaders. Are they supposed to learn about leadership in classrooms or by osmosis? Give them permission to make decisions and fail, and to be accountable.

Program failures are always a teaching moment for anyone involved. I quoted Sir Richard Branson earlier in the book, and he also rightly said that if you are not failing occasionally, you are not trying hard enough to succeed. So, make it a priority to release and delegate control, give the employee who made a great decision the credit in public. You already get credit for being that person's supervisor or business unit leader.

I remember a time in 1984 when a startup airline, also headquartered in Dallas, Muse Air, was giving us fits competitively. They assigned seats, offered all non-smoking flights, and provided other passenger benefits. They announced that they would be initiating service to Little Rock, Arkansas, in six months.

Southwest's senior leadership had had enough of Muse Air nipping at our heels. So, as I recall it, Herb Kelleher told the employee group through his senior team that he wanted Southwest to open in Little Rock in 90 days or less. Nothing fires up airline employees like announcing a new city!

However, you do not just start scheduling 737s on a date you decide. There are complexities to be resolved, such as route slots to be approved by the FAA, concourse space, ticket counters, baggage claim, ramp area with two or three gates with safe spacing. Gate/landing fee contracts have to be negotiated with the airport, and equipment must be ordered and built. You need employees hired and trained.

This was a big request, and Herb was questioned as to the feasibility. What was his response? "You'll figure it out, I trust you." And that was the extent of his involvement in day-to-day planning and execution of the plan. A very agile employee group rose to the occasion and opened Little Rock in record time.

There were many creative and fresh stories from the various departments like facilities, marketing, purchasing, and dispatch. What I will share on the employee hiring and training challenge is that we took a couple of employees from each station, and they served as the opening airport operations team. New hires worked alongside these experienced warriors getting on-the-job training.

At that point, I had only been with Southwest Airlines a little over a year and already felt like we could not be stopped or beaten by any airline. And the entire employee group felt the same. It was a beautiful thing to see. *Postscript:* Muse Air never did open in Little Rock. Soon after that, Muse Air, which had struggled financially since its startup, agreed to be acquired by Southwest.

Tell your employees what the cause and objective is, and release control to your employees to execute as they determine. If they stub their proverbial toe here and there, so what? They will have accomplished the task, learned a great deal about themselves, and boosted their self-confidence. From any failures, they will have learned what they would do differently next time.

THE 7TH PILLAR

Exercise the Power of Praise

Praising another person seems like it should be natural in our DNA. Yet, we seem to praise our pets more than we do our spouses, companions, children, or employees. I do have a working theory that comes as no surprise to most. We become so familiar and close in our personal family and work relationships, we forget to praise, or we delay praise for something monumental.

Simply put, we start taking advantage of the close daily contact and take the relationship for granted. It is not from lack of caring or love; we've forgotten what should have been an ingrained habit. It seems like practices of holding doors open for others or thanking restaurant servers tend to fade over time for some of us. Some might argue it depends on the way you were raised. Perhaps, but in my observations over the years, I think it is a practice that was forgotten because it was not reinforced.

Early in my career as a manager, I would intentionally take candidates to breakfast or lunch just to observe how they interacted with restaurant servers, if they engaged them in conversation, and whether they praised the service at the table. This told me volumes about their attitude and leadership development potential.

The quarterly or annual employee review is not sufficient to deliver praise; parsed out every few months makes the praise seem less than 100 percent sincere. Praise should be spontaneous and heartfelt. Deliver praise when the employee least expects it. Do not just say thank you, say why. Elaborate on the nature and origin of the praise. It will have a more positive impact on that employee's morale and their relationship with you than the formal review could ever have.

Let's get back to the practice of praising as developing a natural habit. When I performed a self-examination on the matter, I noticed that I was good at routinely praising restaurant or fast-food servers, but not very good at routinely praising employees or peers. Without making excuses, it seems I allowed the demands of my schedule and projects to distract me from praising my work-family frequently. Praise should be given not just for achieving a goal or hitting some metric--it should also occur as ongoing gratitude for being part of the team.

To forge a new habit for myself, I began routinely praising strangers and behind the scenes workers. For instance, I would ask the manager of the restaurant if I could say hello and thank-you to the dishwashers. They rarely get praise from the public they serve.

I will say something to the custodial worker in an airport restroom about appreciating his work and let him know I thought it might be the most critical job in the airport. I also say something to the grocery bagger who also retrieves the carts--a thankless job in the hot Arizona summer. It is fantastic how they light up.

And you know what is even more amazing? You feel good for having said something and seeing the impact on someone's day. Complimenting strangers is not natural for most of us, but if you make an effort, you will build neurological muscle memory that will create automatic triggers of praise.

I promise you will also end your day feeling better about yourself for having done so. I have occasionally wondered about the airport custodian who went home after his shift and maybe said to his spouse, "The strangest thing happened at work today. Some guy came up to me while I was mopping the floor and said how he appreciated the job I was doing. It was really nice to hear it and be acknowledged."

Praise is powerful in any organization. People value appreciation over money. All research says so!* (I've listed a few in the back of the book).

EPILOGUE

I have been blessed in my journey to have been personally associated with two distinguished and highly regarded organizational cultures—the United States Army and Southwest Airlines (they have more notoriety than my beloved A-Team). I have endeavored to share and implement the core guiding principles from these two storied and respected organizations in subsequent company leadership roles and my own small businesses. They have afforded me lifelong relationships and success beyond any aspirational goals I may have had.

As I was finishing the last two chapters of the book, the Covid-19 pandemic was unfolding, and our country's economy was grinding to a halt with quarantines and physical distancing. I have been astonished and heartbroken by the reports of sudden and immediate layoffs by businesses within a week or two of the state and federal stay-at-home mandates.

Short-term layoffs leaving employees with no income, and no time to prepare for such, suggests that these businesses had insufficient liquidity, or what we call on Main Street, "operating reserves", to sustain fixed expenses and employee payroll. This book was not meant to be about business financial practices, other than my advocacy for success sharing and profit-sharing as a powerful instrument to an unbeatable company culture.

That said, there is a critical link between a company's ability to weather a financial crisis and the glue that gives The 7 Pillars of this book unbeatable power. ALL companies, whether not-for-profit, small cap to large cap, privately held or publicly traded, should aspire to have 12 months of monthly fixed expenses as an operating reserve for a crisis. Yes, even small family-owned businesses should aim for this. You can do this if you discipline yourself and your company to commit one cent of every revenue dollar to the operating reserve until you have the required reserve balance.

Perhaps I can persuade you to change your perspective by changing your field of vision. It was your idea, possibly your own startup capital, and personal painstaking 80-hour weeks that got your company off the ground and to its present-day success. But unless you are a sole proprietor, as you grew your business, you hired employees to get you to that next level and the next, and the next.

The employees are doing the heavy lifting that affords your increase in personal income (or shareholder income), your lifestyle, wealth building, as well as the curation of your legacy. The employees are your work-family, and their toils are the reason you have what you have. Sure, you pay them a wage for their toils. That just means they come to work, do their job. But a job is a job, not a cause they can get excited about and a philosophy they can embrace. Your success depends on them being committed and willing to vault over speedbumps thrown at your company.

If you commit to exploring the ideas that I lay out in this book for transforming your company culture, and integrate them along with a profit-sharing component, I am more than confident your storehouse will be overflowing. Your company will be unbeatable in the face of competitive headwinds or crisis. Your work-family will make sure of it!

NOTES

The 1ˢᵗ Pillar

LUV NY Stock Exchange Ticker symbol for Southwest Airlines and used as a brand definition of affection throughout the company history

The 2ⁿᵈ Pillar

In 1985 Southwest failed to increase its net profit over the prior year. Southwest Airlines net profit 1985 vs. 1984. https://bit.ly/3f0zKk4

POS Positively Outrageous Service, see The 3ʳᵈ Pillar below.

Zillow-Turn the lights on: https://bit.ly/2YehzjU

The 3ʳᵈ Pillar

Lead with LUV: A Different Way to Create Real Success, by Ken Blanchard and Colleen C. Barrett, 2010, for numerous references in Chapter 3 and elsewhere in the book.

POS Positively Outrageous Service. Created by T. Scott Gross and adopted by Southwest Airlines: https://bit.ly/2MzncnB

Southwest Airlines has never failed to make a net profit in any year since its inception: https://bit.ly/377zyNb

2016 Interview on CNBC with CEO Gary Kelly: https://cnb.cx/3dBVPFc

Herb Kelleher quote: https://bit.ly/2AO5N7M

The 6ᵗʰ Pillar

ToMo: Hold a reflection huddle with your team once a week. 1) Play: What did I learn this week? 2) Purpose: What impact did I have this week? And 3) Potential: What do I want to learn next week? Explaining the why behind the work of your team. One executive at a retail store told us she often introduced a new project by saying, "We have to do this because Linda [the boss] asked for it." This was motivating through emotional pressure, which was hurting her team's performance. So, she started explaining why a project would help the customer instead.

Lindsay McGregor is the co-author of the *New York Times* Bestseller, *Primed to Perform,* and the co-founder and CEO of Vega Factor, a technology and consulting firm.

Neel Doshi is the co-author of the *New York Times* Bestseller, *Primed to Perform,* and the co-founder of Vega Factor. Previously, Neel was a Partner at McKinsey & Company, and the CTO of Genesant Technologies and Technology Director of Finance.com.

The 7th Pillar

All research says so:

Psychology Today, 2013: https://bit.ly/2zgAsuk

Gallup, 2016: https://bit.ly/3eVQmJJ

Entrepreneur 2015: https://bit.ly/2XIenOK

ABOUT THE AUTHOR

Raised in Annapolis,
Maryland until the age
of 15, Dennis Campbell
(DC) lived in
Heidelberg, Germany,
for seven years in the
1970s. Heidelberg,
home of the oldest
university in Germany
(14th Century), which
hosted Mark Twain as a
guest lecturer in the
19th Century, is credited
by DC as having the
most significant
influence on his world
lens and interest in world history.

He served in the United States Army (1976-1980) in the
Military Police Corps, and as an Army Investigator assigned
to undercover drug suppression operations in Germany,
receiving the Army Commendation Medal for record
narcotics seizures, among other accomplishments.

Following military service, DC became known for turning
around anemic organizations, and as a champion of
organizational culture, as the Director of Operations for a
general aviation company in El Paso, Texas, airport
customer service supervisor (El Paso) and territory Sales
and Marketing Manager (Albuquerque, NM) at Southwest
Airlines, Vice President of Sales and Marketing at Visit
Albuquerque, General Manager at the New Mexico State
Fair (the fifth largest in the country at the time), and the
Master Real Estate Broker for the second-largest Ashley

HomeStore licensee in the United States. For record sales in convention development by the A-Team, he was recognized by the Mayor of Albuquerque for his contributions to triple-digit growth in tourism for the city, and the company received the New Mexico Chapter of the American Marketing Association, Marketer of the Year award in 1991.

He has volunteered on various boards and committees, including Ski New Mexico Association, Visit Albuquerque, New Mexico Chapter of Cystic Fibrosis, Meeting Professionals International (MPI) Global Marketing Committee, and Arizona Chapter Board for MPI. He co-founded a foundation supporting an English language program for children in a small village outside of Siem Reap, Cambodia. DC holds a Master Certificate in Hospitality Management from Cornell University and currently belongs to the National Speakers Association, MPI, and National Association of Realtors. He's also a regular volunteer at his church helping in the parking lots and crosswalks for the first impressions team.

An avid scuba diver and PADI certified instructor, he lived on Grand Cayman for two years, enjoying the culture and slower pace of island life while working for Bob Soto's Diving.

Currently residing in Phoenix, Arizona, in addition to his professional speaking and business consulting services for corporate culture, EQ (emotional intelligence), and tourism-related topics, DC has owned an Arizona Real Estate Brokerage firm since 2003, and since 2016 served as a State of Arizona Certified Instructor for real estate pre-licensing and Broker licensing courses, occasionally teaching as an adjunct instructor at an Arizona real estate school.

His hobbies have included flying as a private pilot, racing cars (Porsche 944), tennis, travel with his soulmate, time with his grandchildren, and with his furry companion, Kenzie, a clever Australian Shepherd.

PROFESSIONAL SERVICES

- Keynote speaker
- Private or conference breakout workshops
- Panel facilitation
- Coaching/training
- Business consulting
- Tourism econometrics and feasibility
- Expert witness

If you are interested in learning more about DC's services, we would be honored to explore how we can be of assistance.

Phone: 602-402-6665

Email: dcampbell@campbellra.com

Web: https://dennis-campbell.com

LinkedIn: https://www.linkedin.com/in/dec5871/

Facebook: https://www.facebook.com/DCKeynote